SWEETLY SINGS
THE
DONKEY

SWEETLY SINGS THE DONKEY

ANIMAL ROUNDS FOR
CHILDREN TO SING
OR PLAY ON RECORDERS
SELECTED BY
JOHN LANGSTAFF
PICTURES BY
NANCY WINSLOW PARKER

A Margaret K. McElderry Book

ATHENEUM 1976 NEW YORK

Library of Congress Cataloging in Publication Data

Langstaff, John M   Sweetly sings the donkey.
"A Margaret K. McElderry book."
Summary: A collection of animal rounds for
children to sing and play.
1. Children's songs. [1. Songs]
I. Parker, Nancy Winslow. II. Title.
M1997.L29S95   784'.6'24   76-9530
ISBN 0-689-50063-7

"Dormy Dormouse," words by Kenneth Simpson.
Reprinted from *A First Round Book* with permission of
Novello & Company Ltd., England.

Text copyright © 1976 by John Langstaff
Illustrations copyright © 1976 by Nancy Winslow Parker
All rights reserved
Published simultaneously in Canada by
McClelland & Stewart, Ltd.
Manufactured in the United States of America
Printed by Connecticut Printers, Inc., Hartford
Bound by A. Horowitz & Sons/Bookbinders
Clifton, New Jersey
First Edition

TO MY YOUNG SINGING FRIENDS
and those who play recorders
and other instruments

Here are some easy rounds for singing or playing together. It's a lot of fun to make music this way. First, everyone learns the same simple song. Sing or play it over and over until each of you knows it really well. Then one of you starts and the others follow in turn, coming in at the places marked by numbers 2, 3 and 4 at asterisks printed in brown on the music. When everyone is singing or playing his or her own part, all the voices fit together like a beautiful, intricate puzzle. If you have enough singers, put more than one voice on each part to help one another, like a team for a game. If you don't sing too loudly, you will hear the other parts as well as your own. These rounds can first be sung in two parts. Then, as you get to know them better, try them in the three or four parts intended. You can make the round last as long as you wish; just decide how many times everybody will sing or play it through. The rounds can end in the order they begin, with the last voice-part to enter being the last one to finish, alone.

JOHN LANGSTAFF

SWEETLY SINGS THE DONKEY

Sweet-ly sings the don - key   as he goes to hay.

2.* If   you do   not hold   him,   he will run   a - way.

3.* Kee'yi   Kee'yo   Kee'yi Kee'yo Kee'yay

4.* Kee'yi   Kee'yo   Kee'yi Kee'yo Kee'yay.

WHERE IS JOHN?

Czechoslovakian

Where is John? The old red hen has left her pen.

2.* Where is John? The cows are in the corn a - gain. Oh,

3.* John! _____

THE SNAKE

Marshall Barron, 1975

The snake in sleep - y sun - light lies;

2.* then, hiss - ing, slides a - cross the grass,

3.* I see his scales and shin - y eyes,

4.* and stand a - side to let him pass.

7

THE WOODCHUCK

Pat Shaw, 1973

How much wood would a

2.*
wood - chuck chuck if a

3.*
wood - chuck could chuck

4.*
wood? Oh,

just as much wood as a

wood-chuck could chuck if a wood - chuck could chuck

END HERE
wood. Now tell me . . .

CAT IN THE PLUMTREE

English, 1609

La - dy, come

2.*
down and see, the

3.*
cat sits in the

4.*
plum tree!

A CUCKOO AND AN OWL

French

We hear the night owl call-ing from for-est still and dark, while

from the tall-est oak tree the cuc-koo an-swers back:

2.*

Cuc - koo, cuc - koo, cuc - koo, cuc-koo, cuc - koo. Cuc -

koo, cuc - koo, cuc - koo, cuc-koo, cuc - koo.

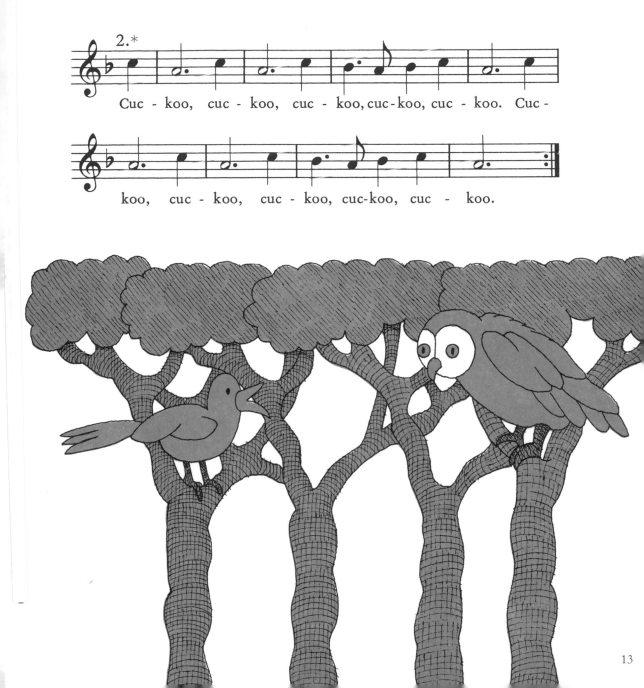

PUSSYCAT, PUSSYCAT

Marshall Barron, 1975

Pus - sy - cat, pus - sy - cat, where have you been?

2.* I've been to Lon - don to vis - it the Queen.

3.* Pus - sy - cat, pus - sy - cat, what did you there? I

4.* fright-ened a lit - tle mouse un - der her chair.

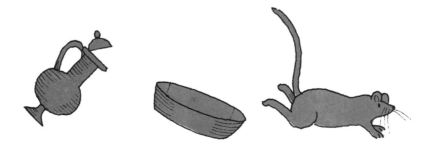

DORMY DORMOUSE

Scottish
Words by Kennett Simpson

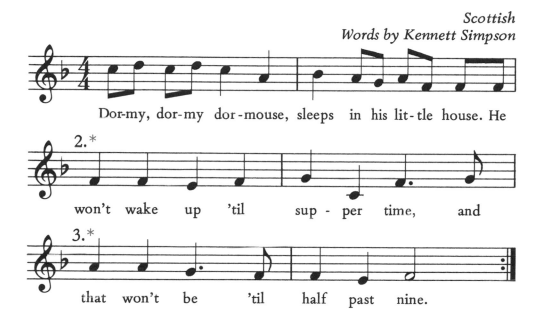

Dor-my, dor-my dor-mouse, sleeps in his lit-tle house. He

2.*

won't wake up 'til sup - per time, and

3.*

that won't be 'til half past nine.

POOR ALGY

Pat Shaw, 1973

Al - gy met a bear; the

2.* bear met Al - gy; the

3.* bear was bul - gy; the

4.* bulge was Al - gy!

MY GOOSE AND THY GOOSE

English

Why does-n't my goose

2.* sing as well as thy goose

3.* when I paid for my goose

4.* twice as much as thou?

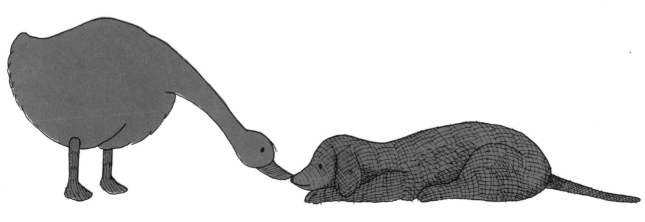

DONKEYS LOVE CARROTS

Belgian

Don - keys love to munch on car - rots,

2.*

Car - rots don't like that at all.

3.*

Hee - haw, hee - haw,

4.*

Lis - ten to the don - key's call.

A LAME, TAME CRANE

Matthew White, 1614

My dame hath a lame, tame crane,

2.* my dame hath a crane that is lame.

3.* Pray gen-tle Jane, let my dame's lame, tame

4.* crane feed and come home a - gain.

25

LOCK THE DAIRY DOOR!

Pat Shaw, 1973

Lock the dai - ry door ___

2.* lock the dai - ry door

3.* "Chic - kle, chac - kle, chee, I

4.* have - n't got the key."

INDEX